Money Wisdom

Money
Wisdom

Carolyn Temsi

∽ AND ∽

Caro Handley

Hodder & Stoughton

First published in Great Britain in 2001 by Hodder and Stoughton
A division of Hodder Headline

A Hodder & Stoughton paperback

British Library Cataloguing in Publication Data

Temsi, Carolyn
Money wisdom
1. Finance, Personal
I. Title II. Handley, Caro
332'.024

ISBN 0 340 76549 6

Typeset by Palimpsest Book Production Limited,
Polmont, Stirlingshire
Printed and bound in Great Britain by
Mackays of Chatham PLC, Chatham, Kent

Hodder and Stoughton
A division of Hodder Headline
338 Euston Road
London NW1 3BH

For John Stevens, our talented accountant.

Our Story

W e're best friends who met when we were both hard-working single mums. Carolyn was a marketing consultant running her own business and Caro was a journalist writing for women's magazines. We met through a mutual interest in humanistic psychotherapy and found that we had a lot in common. Both of us were combining our work with bringing up a young child alone, while being in a very similar financial situation.

We both earned good salaries but had very little idea how to manage money. Both of us were struggling with huge financial responsibilities. We had large debts and had been paying for poor quality financial advice. We were caught in the trap of having homes that were bigger than we needed and could comfortably afford. And we were both working long hours to pay for childcare that was essential because we worked long hours! We were also paying expenses for people who were close to us who were actually not our responsibility.

We realised that we were unable to enjoy the benefits of being high earners as we were stuck in an endless loop of debt and mismanagement. We both knew that we had good organisational and financial skills because we used them in our work where we were successful and respected. Yet we'd both been better off when we were earning small salaries in our first jobs and life was simpler.

Together we made a commitment to learning about money, to understand what we were doing wrong and how we could make changes resulting in real and lasting benefits. We were determined to understand the emotional, spiritual and psychological aspects of money as well as the practical skills. We wanted to make sure that we enjoyed the way that we earned our money, that we balanced our lives more effectively, that we got to spend more time with our children and new partners and that we lived in abundance.

The lessons along the way were tough, challenging, exciting, frustrating but always enriching. We helped ourselves and each other and developed a totally new understanding of money.

We have written this book for ourselves, our partners, our children and for you. We hope that our wisdom enriches your journey to financial enlightenment and that your life is filled with peace, joy and plenty.

Introduction

We believe that we all deserve financial security, abundance and the skills and confidence to manage money in our lives.

We believe that this is your right.

Money Wisdom is here to guide and advise you, whether you're good with money or struggling to make ends meet.

Whether you're rich or poor, able to draw money to you or letting it go too easily, *Money Wisdom* will answer your questions, and set you on the path which feels satisfying, enriching and right for you.

We have used the wisdom in this book to learn how to manage money in our own lives in a way which is joyful and rewarding. We want to share this wisdom with as many people as possible, so that you too may experience the riches and success that you deserve.

We wish you well.

How to use this book

Here is some guidance on how to form your question:

    keep it simple,
    ask for guidance and advice about your question rather than
       yes/no answers,
    ask only what you are willing to have answered.

If you want *Money Wisdom* to help you, it means:

    treating it with care and respect,
    taking your time rather than rushing,
    being willing to accept the advice offered,
    opening yourself up to the possibility of change,
    actively engaging in whatever it requires of you,
    accepting the answers, whatever they may be.

If you want a more detailed answer open the book three times
while thinking of your question.

    The first page will refer to the present moment, the second to
the immediate future, the third to the long-term future.

Cost

When you open this book here, it is time to focus on the price you pay for your money. How do you make your money or from whom do you receive it? What does this entail? What does it ask of you? Are you happy and satisfied with the activities in which you engage to make money? Are you comfortable at a mental, emotional and moral level? How much time and effort does your money-making require? You need to question whether what you do, how you do it and the way you feel about doing it, is actually worth the financial benefits this brings to you.

Something is out of balance. The price is too high or the consequences are too great. Perhaps you are being offered money as a gift or a loan. This tells you to look at the bigger cost rather than just focusing on the short term. What will it cost you in the long run? Who will you be indebted to? How will you feel about this? Will this transaction create stress? If so, recognise this as a part of the cost. Maybe you need to think again.

Look at what you spend your money on and put this against what it took from you to create that money. Then decide whether the end result was worth what you went through to get this. This is the real cost of any spending, to you. It's about lifestyle, effort and the consequences rather than about pounds or dollars.

Now is the time to clearly define how many hours you work for each item you spend money on. Keep a record of all of your spending for a day or a week or better still for a month and then decide whether this feels like a good way to be spending your money. Those things that you truly value can be valued all the more when you realise the effort that you committed to gaining them and you'll quickly spot where you waste your money and so will be able to address this.

Remember to look at the cost of money around your friendships and relationships. Do you feel used or overburdened when you have riches to share or are you dependent and resentful because you rely too heavily on someone else to support you? Dependency has its own huge cost. If you look at the big picture, would it cost you less overall, to provide your own income?

The price of money is linked to the value that you give to yourself. This is why you need to address this issue now. Doing so will change your life.

Honesty

When you open this book here, it asks you to be honest about your financial position, with both yourself and others. Honesty is always the best policy.

Are you trying to kid yourself or someone else that things are other than they are? If this description doesn't seem to fit with your position right now, dig a little deeper to establish where you're fudging or clouding the issues. Be honest with yourself and you'll know what this refers to.

Maybe you have the opportunity to benefit financially from a situation that requires some level of dishonesty. It may simply be the need for you to turn a blind eye, feign ignorance or lie by omission. Say 'no' and take the honest approach. Be scrupulous, no matter how sorely you are tempted. However you behave now will come back to you in the future. Only honesty will be rewarded.

Sit down with a pen and paper and work through your income and your outgoings. Get clear about where you spend your money and about your true financial position. Write down all your debts and any savings. What is the honest picture? Are you comfortable about this? What are you going to do about it?

You need to define a realistic, achievable solution to your financial position. Are you honest about your requirements? Will you really not survive without your next planned purchase? Are your goals realistic? It's easy to overstretch ourselves in our current 'have it all' society. You are only truly rich when you consistently spend less than you have. Is this what you are doing?

Part of honesty is about being willing to really face our overspending. Are you spending more than you actually have? Are you gambling without monitoring the amount you spend or in the hope that this will solve your financial future? Honesty means admitting that most gamblers lose, particularly the needy ones. It's time to stop.

You also need to look at how honest you are with others about your financial position. Are you worried that you will be judged if you let people know the extent of your savings or debt. You have the right to privacy, but should have no need for secrecy. Be proud of who you are and the money you have.

Honesty is about being genuine and riches cannot be built on any other foundation. Go on, get honest. It pays!

Relax

When you open this book here, it is a welcome relief. It means that you can rest easy and know that, at this moment in your life, you're not meant to be worrying about money. Instead, it tells you that you should take a break from anxiety, work or effort. That you need to be less tense and rigid and that you need to unbend and soften.

For those of you who will cheer and happily get on with other things, this must sound great. Maybe your finances are in a really good state at the moment and if this is the case know that it's time to relax and enjoy your money. If not, know that things should soon improve. Without being irresponsible it's time to relax about it.

For those of you who are very caught up in concerns around money right now, the advice to relax may sound crazy, irrelevant or irresponsible. Know that it is not. This is the advice that you need and you're going to have to trust it before anything will change for the better.

How do you relax? Start with your breathing. Breathe in deeply through your nose but imagine that the air is coming in through your coccyx at the base of your spine. At an energetic level this is where we hold our fears. In order to release them we actually have to accept them and we can do this by simply being with our feelings when we breathe like this. It really is going to be OK.

Go for a walk, read a book, meet friends, do whatever works for you. Leave the money to a force greater than yourself. It will look after it far better without your interference. Without being reckless, believe that whatever money worries or financial issues you have will soon resolve themselves. You cannot speed up this process. Know that solutions we can't foresee turn up all the time. It is when we stop needing to know everything that we leave space for the unforeseen to enter our lives. If you catch yourself tensing and thinking about money again, be nice to yourself but remind yourself that you are off duty right now. Just come back to your breathing and relaxing and it will pass.

Financial resolution may take some time, but in the meantime, rest easy. You have permission to trust that all is well. All is well.

Be Yourself

When something is authentic, it is exactly what it claims to be. It is the genuine article. You open this book here when you need to be directed towards a more authentic representation of yourself. Because, in order for money to flow into your life, you need to operate in a manner which is congruent with who you really are and who you want to be.

Too often we find that money seems to flow towards those who are not authentic. It can seem that the best sales people are those who don't really care whether they sell the genuine article or have satisfied customers. But this isn't actually true. Real wealth goes to those who are genuine. People who get rich at the expense of others lose their money just as quickly. If you really want money to flow into your life you have to be your real self and that means caring about yourself and the other people around whom your money is made.

Do what you enjoy doing. This is the true route to riches. When we do that which brings us pleasure, we do it with a good heart and we do it well. Focus on where the overlap is between what you love to do and financial viability. What skills do you have that others would pay for? What do you enjoy that could lead you into a far more relevant profession?

If you love the outdoors you don't have to sit in an office. Become a postman or a forest ranger, walk dogs or train as a landscape gardener! The options are endless but they all start with you letting yourself be who you really are. Trust that the money will go hand in hand with your higher level of authenticity.

You may need to look at how you hide your real self for fear that those who employ you or pay you won't find the real you acceptable. You don't have to pretend to be someone else any more. Remember that those people who don't really value you shouldn't be dictating how you live your life. The people who do value you have been drawn to your inner core, not the persona that you cloak yourself in, so let them have more of what they really want. This in turn will lead to greater value being placed upon you and so the money will flow.

Start putting more of yourself into the way that you earn or receive your income as well as into the way that you spend it. Put more goodwill into your efforts and really mean what you say and do. As you feel more genuine your satisfaction levels will rise and you will be rewarded.

Life will reward you as long as you are true to yourself. Now is the time.

Greed

When you open this book here, it offers you a warning. Greed must be operating somewhere in your life and affecting your money situation.

Pay close attention, as it needs to be nipped in the bud. No good can ever come from greed.

Being greedy is about consuming, desiring or hanging on to something in excess of our real needs. Sometimes we know that this is exactly what we are doing and other times we don't. But it doesn't make any difference.

When we have worked hard to gain something or benefited unexpectedly and are in the throes of enjoying this, it can be very hard to rein ourselves in and to know that we've had enough. Sadly, enjoying something often leads to an unwillingness to let it end. But then we get stuck. We get greedy. We want more, we want it all and the energy we create by being greedy is then guaranteed to bring about loss.

Implicit in greed is the notion that there won't be enough to go around or for you to get the share that you desire. Behind it is a belief in poverty rather than abundance. The need for excess in the present shows your lack of trust in the future. You don't need to be greedy; there will be enough.

Don't fall into the trap of trying to fill a feeling of inner emptiness with physical and material things. It doesn't work and we just get more and more greedy in the process. Greed is very tied up with materialism. It makes physical things like cash and possessions more important than spirituality and emotional peace. Look at how you are prioritising these issues in your life and pay more attention to them.

Is what you have and what you can get more important to you than who you are? If this is so then know that others will see you in the same way. Have you fallen into the trap of trying to own the right object or have a particular experience without realising that the pleasure it will bring won't stop you needing to deal with your underlying feelings? Enjoy your material possessions but don't become a slave to them and judge yourself or expect others to judge you by them.

Remember generosity. Know that you really can't take it with you when you pass on. Trust that there is enough for everyone, including you, now and in the future. It is ironic, but when we are greedy we isolate ourselves and block the flow of wealth. The person who rejects greed is the one who prospers. Open up and share and you'll find that it works.

Persistence

When you open this book here, the issue you need to face is persistence. Maybe you're saving towards something special, trying to get out of debt or attempting to get a new idea off the ground. You need persistence to focus steadfastly on your goal and to refuse to be dissuaded, by yourself or others.

On the other hand, perhaps you are being too persistent about financial issues and making life unnecessarily difficult. Are you hanging onto money you need to free up, or putting yourself or others under pressure to behave in a certain way? If so it's time to let go of this approach and trust that all will be well when you do.

Perhaps you are giving up too early or too easily. Have you been putting time and effort into something that doesn't seem to be paying off? Are you surprised that it is turning out to require more from you than you anticipated, to accomplish what you hoped for? They say that the best inventions are 2 percent inspiration and 98 percent perspiration. You need to realise that the combination of continued effort and commitment are the prerequisites to success. It's easy to have the idea, the challenge is in seeing it through and actually making it happen.

True persistence takes courage. You need to judge whether something just needs enough time and continued effort to come to fruition or if you are banging your head against a brick wall. Sometimes a new angle or approach is required and you may have to try things a number of different ways before you get it right. Sometimes it means going back to the drawing board over and over again. Be willing to pick yourself up and dust yourself off and carry on.

Maybe you need to take a break and come back to it refreshed. Remember that the most effective persistence makes good use of the feedback you get along the way. This is real tenacity. Stop and take a good look at which bits are working and which bits aren't. Often being too close to something blinds you. Get an outside opinion. What advice would you give to someone else or want them to give you?

Don't listen to anyone who tries to dissuade you. Persistence assures you that your success is guaranteed as long as you don't give in and you don't give up. You can do it.

Completion

When you open this book here it tells you that you need to see something through properly to its real end in order to gain success and balance in your financial life.

It's so easy to start something and then get distracted or drawn away before we finish it. But the trouble with this is that it then leaves us like children, running around with our shoelaces left undone. Sooner or later they will trip us up. Then, because what we don't finish is often invisible or intangible, we can't easily see where the difficulties are coming from.

When you fail to complete things properly you waste your energy unnecessarily. It's as if each ending left unfinished is a thread connected to your wealth. The money trickles away in an unforeseen manner, finding an easy exit route, like water running down ropes. Also, these loose invisible threads hang around you, ready to tangle themselves into any new business. Life becomes a clutter and a muddle.

What is needed is a financial clearing. Then you contain your energy in a tidy manner, without allowing it to leak and dissipate all around you. Concentrate on following through what you have begun. If you're on a particular path you need to just get on with it and keep on doing it until you finish. Deal with the detail. Dot your I's and cross your T's. Tie up all loose ends and then put it away in an organised manner so you know where you are if you ever need to come back to it.

Sort out your paperwork, streamline your accounting system, close any old accounts, pay off any outstanding debts, free money that is tied up too tightly and get up to date. Have you checked whether the way you handle your money still fits with your needs? How many habits and systems are just old ways that you haven't updated?

Completion is telling you that now is the time to finish with something financially instead of continuing. Has something run its course? What has gone on for longer than you anticipated and is no longer beneficial to you? When we don't finish what we should, it doesn't leave us free to start something new. When one door closes, another one opens, not the other way around. Close the door and have faith that new will come into your life and be of benefit financially.

Don't undertake something that you won't be able to finish. Make sure that you can properly complete whatever you start, even if it means that you can take less on. By bringing things to their desired and appropriate endings, you will prosper.

Guidance

When you open this book here, it is to let you know that you need help with your finances. You are not getting the support that you deserve and require. Because money is a private issue we often end up operating in a vacuum, isolating ourselves without even realising that this is what we are doing.

When things are going well we often don't realise that with outside input, they could go even better. When things are going badly, we are unlikely to feel comfortable exposing our situation to others. But, now is the time to interrupt your usual pattern and involve an outside influence.

Where do you look for advice and leadership? Who could offer a useful and relevant opinion? Who do you know who is a good role model for you? Talk to others and find out what they do around money. Review which aspects of their approach would be useful for you and set about actually integrating these new ideas into your life.

The best guide is someone who is wiser and more knowledgeable than yourself. This can be a sign that your situation requires the involvement of a specialist and you should not be trying to deal alone with whatever it is. Talk to an expert who can help and advise you. Make sure that this is someone with reliable references, who has already guided another to a successful outcome under similar circumstances. Don't just trust someone blindly, but when you get good advice, take it seriously. Act in the manner necessary to steer your situation to a sound outcome.

Guidance is an ongoing process where you not only set off in the right direction, but you also monitor the journey as you travel. Have you started something that you are no longer guiding with sufficient attention to ensure the best outcome? If so, this asks you to involve yourself, and/or others, much more closely.

Guidance also involves instruction and influence of a more subtle nature. Perhaps now is the time to look for guidance from within. Are you paying proper respect to your intuition? Do you realise that your gut instinct is based on masses of information that you have already gathered but are not currently holding in your consciousness? You know more than you think you know and it is time to trust yourself. Create some space to hear what your own advice is and then take it. Guide yourself.

Remember that each day the answer is always available if we will open ourselves up to be guided.

Struggle

When you open this book here, it is an acknowledgement that money is causing you pain or stress at the moment. Are you suffering from a shortage of cash to meet your needs and commitments? Are you unable to have or to do what you most want at the present time? Are you struggling with a moral dilemma around money? Or are you afraid that others judge you for how much or how little money you have? Something is not working for you and it is time to address this.

Struggle is sometimes a sign that you are in a seemingly powerless position financially. How have you got yourself into this situation and what are you going to do to get out of it? Changing things may not be easy but change is required. Do whatever you can do to move things along.

Worrying about money is depleting your energy. Although you may not be aware of it you are mentally preoccupied and emotionally drained. If you are struggling as a result of neglecting your finances, now is the time to seriously address this situation. If you are very aware of the problems and feel stuck and unable to do something about them then you need to take a different approach.

Money is simply a symbolic representation of other elements in your life. Open out your perspective and start to look at what the real situation is that you are struggling with. What would you be thinking about if it wasn't money? Why are you blocking yourself in this way?

Life was never meant to be a struggle. Our difficulties around money, whether they are because we have too much or too little of it will always have been created or drawn to ourselves for a reason. There is some benefit in this struggle and you need to find out what it is and determine whether you are willing to let go of it.

Put the negatives aside and find the good instead. What do you get from organising yourself in the way that creates struggle? What does it allow you to indulge in or avoid? How does it position you in relation to others? Are you powerful or a hopeless victim, are you able to avoid working or forced to keep working? What would you have to face if the struggle went away? What would you have to do or give up to stop creating the problem?

To struggle is to exert a considerable force against a restriction. So sometimes the most powerful approach is to stop resisting. Go with the pressure rather than against it and you deflate it. Accept your reality. Trust that you are struggling for your own reasons and that you can choose to stop whenever you like. It doesn't matter if this doesn't feel true, know that it is true. Then you regain your power and can choose to end your struggle with money.

Generosity

When you open this book here, the message is beautifully straightforward. Generosity is the art of giving of yourself, freely and with goodwill. In this context it means that you need to be financially generous in an appropriate way. Give of your earnings, wealth, income, savings, winnings or valuables and any of the items or opportunities that result from them.

Generosity carries within it confidence, a belief in abundance and a sense of having enough yourself, so that you are able to share with others. Know that you can afford to be generous right now. When you give, your wealth will come back to you magnified, but only when your motive is to give rather than to be rewarded.

True generosity involves giving to others with no strings attached. With no desire to see that which you give returned to you. You need to do it with a good heart so that you don't end up feeling resentful or trying to keep the person to whom you are being generous indebted to you. Give from the heart rather than the head.

Now is the time to buy that gift, offer that treat or help someone out who is relying on you or who has no one to rely on. Check that you are sufficiently generous with your loved ones as well as with strangers who share this world with you. How much of your income or earning capacity, skill or input goes to charity? How much to good causes? How much to the underprivileged? You don't need to be generous with those who sit back waiting for a handout but there are plenty of people who deserve your help and support or who genuinely can't help themselves. Be generous to yourself too. Treat yourself with the kindness and consideration you would give to someone you love.

Check that you are being generous for the right reasons. What is your agenda? What are you hoping to gain through your generosity, other than to benefit the receiver and to communicate your goodwill. If you find even a hint of an ulterior motive then let it go. Practise giving with no expectations of the outcome. It's a wonderfully liberating experience.

Remember that when you are generous you move your financial energy in an outward direction, you open up. But it is important to balance the giving of your wealth with holding on to it. Your generosity needs to ebb and flow in order to create that balance. You need to give appropriately and not recklessly, quietly, not flamboyantly. Always give with sensitivity and respect so that the gift can be truly appreciated.

Enjoy being generous, it is one of life's great pleasures.

Family Values

When you open this book here, it tells you that you are being strongly influenced by the financial values of your family of origin. These are the lessons and messages that you picked up in the process of growing up. Some of them will have been clear and explicit and others more subtle, perhaps learnt by example, through witnessing actions and attitudes.

Is your family of origin currently involved with or offering opinions on your financial situation? Or is their influence operating more subtly, as you attempt to live according to what you were told or taught?

Now is the time to evaluate those influences clearly and honestly. It's important to realise that your family was influenced by their own family too, and that many of their beliefs would have been tied in with the prevailing conditions and culture. It isn't always good advice just because it comes from within the family and by the same token their advice shouldn't always be dismissed as worthless.

There will probably be some values that you will wish to keep and some that it is time to discard. Sit down and write a list of all the opinions about money and related issues that you can attribute to your family and your upbringing. Were you rich or poor or somewhere in between? Was money respected or feared? Were you brought up to believe in cash, cheque or plastic, in credit, savings or debt? Were you taught that others would judge you for the money you have or don't have?

Do you choose your own bank, accountant and advisors or are you tied in to a previous family arrangement? Do you know much about your money or have you been taught to believe that others should manage your situation?

How dependent are you on your family of origin? Have you grown up and left home yet with regard to your money? Is your family still providing for your basic needs even though you are now an adult? What role do you play in the family in relation to money? Maybe you are the provider, having to work hard to constantly supply others in your family. Look at what this costs you in terms of resentment and lifestyle. Why is this your role? Is this the way that you try to gain love and approval? Or do you keep yourself in a negative financial situation to avoid jealousy from your family?

Now is the time to review all of this and make your own rules. Be an adult, trust your own judgement, develop your own beliefs and enjoy your independence. You are your real family now.

Manifestation

When you open this book here it is time to trust that all is well and that it is in your power to achieve what you want. Manifestation is the act of bringing something from a thought form into physical matter. Making it tangible. For example we wish for some money and, in turn, it arrives. Or we wish for a change of attitude for ourselves or others and we get it. In fact, the more flexible we are about how things can change or turn up physically, the easier it is to create them. Maybe we get a tax rebate, win the lottery or find some money on the street. Maybe we get paid earlier than expected or someone returns a forgotten loan. Or maybe we get more comfortable around our money, or are able to enjoy it in new ways.

Manifestation is one of the most magical and accessible rules of the universe and yet so many of us are unaware of it or don't understand how to harness it for ourselves.

One of the great things about manifestation is that you don't have to believe in it to make it work. But when you practise it and see how it works you can't help but believe in it. Then once you believe, you can use it more effectively.

When you open this book here, it is a sign that something financial is about to manifest in your life. All the indications are good. What you wish for will become present in your life.

The art of manifestation breaks down into a number of basic rules. First, be realistic, start by manifesting small amounts in your life and increase this as your trust in your ability builds. Secondly, know what you want, know what it's for and visualise your life with it. The clearer the picture you can build the greater the success of your manifestation. Thirdly, work for your own good and that of those around you. Avoid being selfish, greedy or negative. It's all out there, looking for a home, trust that there is enough for everyone. Finally, draw it to you; don't go chasing after it. Manifestation comes to those who concentrate and trust. It goes in the opposite direction at the first hint of desperation or panic. Confidence is the key.

The time is right for you to manifest what you need. Make the effort. Don't sit back and wait for the laws of nature to deliver it into your lap. Go out and meet it half way. It works on the principle of 'energy in, energy out'. Even if what you do doesn't pay off directly, the reward will come nevertheless, because you joined in and got things moving.

The power lies with you!

Power

When you open this book here you can be happy because it is time to recognise and value your own power around money.

Power is the ability to act and to influence the people and circumstances around us and right now you are in a very powerful position. We all have the potential for great power, and at this moment your power is strong and clear and vibrant. Take advantage of this perfect timing.

You can use your power in ways that will benefit you and those around you as long as you use it with care, love and respect. What do you want to accomplish? What are your dreams and goals? What have you longed to do and been afraid to try? Now is the time to go for it. Without being reckless or irresponsible rise to the challenge, push yourself forward and know that the limitless power of the universe is yours for the taking.

Now is the time to ask for what you want with the confidence that it will be granted. Speak up loudly and clearly. Trust in your skills and ability to achieve what you set out to. Negotiate from a powerful position knowing that it is possible to satisfy everyone involved. Hold your ground while respecting others. Know that you can be respected in return and take advantage of the huge amount of positive energy available to you.

If you're not feeling powerful right now it is simply because you don't know about your power or you are resisting it for fear of where it will take you. Moving forward brings change, which is always a challenge but with this also comes exciting new possibilities. Know that power, used rightly, is a good thing. Realise that you can control the money in your life. You can make choices and decisions that will take you to where you want to be.

You have the power. Use it.

Comfort

When you open this book here it is because you need to address the way that you use money to comfort yourself.

Comfort is all about feeling both physically and emotionally comfortable. About being safe, warm, content, cosy, satisfied, comforted.

You deserve these things in your life and you can organise your spending in a way that allows you to have these things without creating debt or stress for yourself.

Are you holding on to your money and refusing to use it to give yourself comfort? Or are you indulging in comfort shopping and comfort spending which you hope will make you feel better? Do you find that what you buy doesn't hit the mark and just eats away at your available money?

Be more discerning about what you need. You need things that are directly comforting to your body and soul. Buy a candle, a soft cushion, a warm blanket and something nice for the bath. Allowing yourself to hug a hot water bottle on the sofa in peace and quiet for an hour will bring you far greater rewards than an afternoon at the shopping centre. Perhaps a walk in the woods would bring you comfort, to be amongst nature. Breathe deeply and trust that things are exactly as they are meant to be right now.

When you comfort yourself properly you'll find that you spend your money wisely and your experience of life will be greatly improved. This will bring all-round benefits that will impact on how you organise yourself, your time and your money.

Whatever financial issue you are addressing right now, allow yourself some comfort and you will make your decisions from a far better place. If money is creating stress in your life, take time out to comfort yourself now, rather than waiting for the difficulty to pass.

If your life is always busy as you rush from one thing to another, know that an upturn in your finances will not arise until you slow down and comfort yourself. To do so will restore your energy and feed your soul, leaving you in a far stronger place to draw riches to you.

Relax and enjoy it. You deserve it.

Relationships

When you open this book here it is time to look at the way that the financial issues in your life are affecting your closest relationships.

Unresolved and unbalanced money issues can have a huge impact on your relationships with family, partners and friends. When you can't sort out money matters together, clearly and with agreement then the relationship cannot be truly happy and healthy. Look carefully at the impact money is having on you and your relationships.

Have you borrowed or lent money without a clear agreement about paying it back? Are you supporting others inappropriately, or relying on handouts from a family member that leave you feeling powerless and frustrated? Do you or does your partner handle all the money or make all the financial decisions? Do you keep all of your money hidden or feel bad about having it? These situations leave relationships unclear and uncomfortable, with one or both of you feeling resentful.

If you're pretending that things are fine and ignoring a money issue in one of your relationships it is time to sort it out, with honesty and goodwill.

Take responsibility for this and do it without blame or argument. Be truthful about buried resentments and get clear about the kinds of financial arrangements that will work and leave you both feeling good.

You may also be using money to avoid relationships, rejecting potential partners and friends because they have too much or too little money. If you do this then recognise it for the excuse it is and face the fear that others will reject you, which is what lies behind it.

Don't let money prevent you from having the relationship you want, or cloud the relationships you already have. Money represents energy, and when the energy around money gets stuck it can only put the relationship under pressure and cause unhappiness.

Clear the flow of energy in your relationship by clearing the money issues and enjoy reaping the benefits.

Gift

When you open this book here, it means that you are in the process of receiving or are about to receive a gift that will influence your wealth and prosperity.

A gift involves no obligation or debt. It comes with no strings attached. You may be given cash in some form, a cheque, premium bond, a retail voucher or you may receive an object of some value. Whatever you receive you need to appreciate it and welcome it into your life no matter how small it is.

Remember: 'never look a gift horse in the mouth'. At this stage you cannot know the real impact and value of the gift you receive. Only its surface value. A book token may lead you to a whole new financially rewarding career. A single pound may buy the winning lottery ticket. The gift may be rewarding in its own right or be a stepping stone to greater things.

Enjoy. Accept it as freely given. Appreciate the giver, but know that what you have is now yours to do with as you wish. Ownership has been transferred in the giving. If not, then it is not a true gift.

Sometimes life sends us a gift in the most unexpected shape or form. If you don't see a tangible gift, reflect on what is going on in your life right now and find the gift lurking in the shadows. Has luck come your way recently or is it about to descend on you? Is there an opportunity around that you can turn into a gift for yourself?

Not all gifts come gift-wrapped. Sometimes it is by looking a bit more closely at our lives that we find the gift being offered to us. Sometimes this can be found in the most trying of circumstances. Adversity always carries its own gift and this can be the decision to do things in a different way, or a new, clearer understanding of your situation. Every cloud has a silver lining. If times are difficult know that you opened the book here to direct you to the jewel within all of this that you have so far failed to notice. Something good will come out of it, a change in direction, a chance opportunity, a new set of skills or strengths.

Life is giving you a gift and you will be richer for it. The more of it you can recognise, the more of it you will receive. Simply trust and allow yourself to discover the gift.

Self-Esteem

When you open this book here it is time to look at your self-esteem and the impact it has on your handling of money and your attitudes to money. Self-esteem is the way you feel about yourself and right now your self-esteem is low in at least one area of your life.

Low self-esteem means that you don't feel good about yourself in some way. When you have low self-esteem specifically around money it stops you bringing it into your life, being able to enjoy it or being able to hold on to it. Are you in debt, unable to earn a good salary or struggling to make ends meet? Are you able to attract money but then keep letting it go by giving it away, spending too much on others, wasting it or losing it? Or do you hide your money away or feel guilty about having it?

Know that your patterns around money reflect the value that you give to yourself. The amount you charge for the work you do is a clue to this. With low self-esteem we undervalue what we do. Find out what the going rate is and make sure that anything you do is fairly rewarded.

If you want to change your financial situation you need to

work on your self-esteem. Start to treat yourself in the way that you would treat a good friend. Focus on your strengths and be more forgiving and accepting of what you see as your faults and weaknesses. Nurture yourself and deal with your unresolved childhood pain. Buy a book on self-esteem and investigate therapy or counselling. When your self-esteem improves you will soon see it reflected in your financial situation.

Perhaps your low self-esteem shows itself in your inability to spend money on yourself. Do you make enough money but have no idea that it's OK to spend whatever it takes on yourself to make your life safe, comfortable, relaxed and pleasurable? As you work on your low self-esteem you'll realise that it really is fine to spend your money on yourself, and that you won't be criticised by people who truly care about you.

Raising your self-esteem is the key to financial success. It takes courage and hard work but it's worth it.

Negotiation

When you open this book here it is because you need to bring the art of negotiation into your life around money.

Negotiation is about power sharing, compromise and resolution. It involves listening to and respecting another person's position while holding on to and respecting your own and then being willing to work towards reaching a point at which you can both feel satisfied.

Where, how and with whom do you need to negotiate? Are you resentful or unhappy because someone else has all the power over your money? Are you ignoring and opting out of money matters, leaving them to others to sort out? Are you being over-controlling around money and making decisions you should be sharing with someone else? Or do you need to negotiate a pay rise or new job for yourself?

Whichever it is, you are in an unbalanced situation which can bring you no benefit. Too much or too little power is always unhealthy and unsatisfying. In order to negotiate you need to be clear about what you want and to get clear about what the other person wants. You need to have good communication and make sure that you understand each other. You also need to decide what you will or will not compromise on and be willing to review this as you go along.

Good negotiation results in a win-win situation in which both of you end up satisfied, even if you have given up part of what you wanted.

Avoid bullying, stubbornness, emotional manipulation and blackmail. Negotiate with a healthy expectation that you will both end up happy.

Master the art of negotiation and you will be in a stronger and more successful position financially.

Effort

When you open the book here, it is telling you that effort is required from you in order to improve or resolve your financial situation.

Effort is defined as a mental or physical exertion. It's about you really being willing to do what is needed and about being active and keeping at it rather than taking the easy option.

How much effort have you been putting into your finances? What are you doing to improve your situation? How much time and attention do you pay to how you manage your money and how you make your money? You can't ignore it and assume that it will look after itself because it won't. It's up to you.

Perhaps the effort required involves you clarifying your current and long-term objectives. What exactly do you want? How specific can you be? What are you hoping for? What are you willing to do to realise your dream? Or you may need to put effort into sorting out your financial relationship with another person.

When you have a clear purpose or objective then you can become constructive in bringing it about. Now is the time to stick at it and stick with it. Don't be dissuaded too easily by others. Don't give up when things aren't as easy as you had expected. By putting your own energy into your finances and not being dissuaded then the rewards will really be yours.

Remember that when you are doing what is right for you, then the effort required becomes a type of pleasure. It still demands our time but it comes to us naturally and easily. If the effort that you are exerting leaves you feeling tired and frustrated it may be a good idea to question what you are doing. Maybe it's time to look at things from a different angle. What if you took an alternative approach?

Remember that you need to look after yourself. Your efforts will be more productive if they are part of an overall healthy balanced life.

Finally keep in mind that all of your efforts are for you, so remember to enjoy yourself. There's nothing like the reward of energy well spent and when you make the effort this will be yours along with an upturn in your finances.

Avoidance

When you open this book here, it means that money is not the real issue in your life right now, it only seems that it is. This can be very hard to accept, particularly if you are struggling with financial difficulties or important decisions. But, by accepting this, you will be able to release some of the hold that money has over you and deal with the more crucial underlying issues.

When we focus on money as if it is the real issue, we do so to avoid putting the focus where it really belongs. Often what we have is a sense of anxiety or fear. We're not really sure what these feelings are about or where they come from so we then attach these feelings to our financial situation. By doing this we provide ourselves with something tangible to worry about. We can convince ourselves that by controlling and influencing our financial situation then the uncomfortable feelings will go away. But even if they do the feelings will soon return because this approach only ever offers a temporary fix. The underlying anxiety still exists and persists.

When you open the book at Avoidance it is actually offering you liberation. It is showing you that there is another way to feel safe, secure and comfortable and that this doesn't rely on how much money you do or don't have. Forget about the money and just have the feeling that is below all of the rationalising and thinking. You don't have to act on it, just have it. What is it?

Do you feel scared, tired, lonely, insecure, sad or anxious? Do you feel bored, angry, dissatisfied? What was money meant to do for you that isn't happening? Are you sick of trying to fix your life? Give up this way of thinking because your need to fix things is based on the desire to make the feelings go away and it's a thankless task. You have to work through the feelings to come to the other side.

If you didn't have money to worry about who would you be? You would have to let those old anxieties and fears drift to the surface and let them stick around. It is only by being brave enough to be with the painful feelings that you are trying to avoid, that you will be free of them.

Let the feelings come up. They really won't be as bad as you might fear. It's avoiding them that is so painful and stressful. It's time to stop avoiding.

Beyond avoidance comes the strength and courage to sort out the money issues in your life so that you are satisfied and happy.

Prosperity

When you open the book at this page, it is a blessing. It means that good fortune shines down upon you and radiates into your life. Know that you are favoured right now. Financial prosperity is on its way to you if it hasn't recently arrived. Your destiny is favourable.

This is the right time to buy a lottery ticket or try your hand at a small investment. It encourages you to trust that the odds are on your side and that Lady Luck shines upon you.

However, be wary of irresponsibility and recklessness or being mean or tight around money. These are not rewarded. Be ready to open your heart to prosperity, because it cannot make itself at home where it is not welcomed and trusted. If you believe that any prosperity is too good to be true, then it will quickly move on to someone who is more accepting. It is important to welcome even the smallest examples of prosperity, in order to lay the path for greater prosperity to follow in its tracks. If you see a penny in the street, stop and pick it up and be grateful. If someone gives you something you weren't expecting or acts in a generous way recognise that this is the beginning of your current wave of prosperity.

Prosperity will mean different things to different people, and the clearer you are about what it means to you, the greater chance you have of seeing the successful accomplishment of your financial dreams. Maybe you will get a pay rise, or your property will suddenly develop a large amount of equity. Maybe you are due for a tax rebate or a financial judgement in your favour. Expect good fortune and that is what you will get.

With prosperity there are two rules to remember. One is never to be cynical or ungrateful for what comes your way. It may not be what you expected but it may be all that your subconscious is comfortable with right now. See every opportunity as a chance to practise embracing prosperity and watch your fortunes rise. The second rule is that prosperity comes to you, you can't go after it. The harder you chase it, the further it slips away. It moves in the opposite direction from desperation and need. So, stand your ground and trust that it will find you. You can encourage it by exuding confidence and self-assurance.

Prosperity is your right at this moment in time. Know this and it will find you.

Energy

When you open this book here, know that money is simply energy. This is the basic principle that underlies all financial issues in our world.

It's time to take advantage of this knowledge now and to do this you have to understand, or be reminded of, the concept of energy.

From a scientific perspective all matter, all existence, everything is simply a mass of vibrating energy. Air, trees, humans, tables and chairs are all different forms of energy. Each is made up of atomic particles that move around in constant motion. Some seem solid, like a table or a wall, but only because they contain energy in a more dense and slow-moving form. Some seem more ethereal, such as water or air. But they are just forms of energy. Remember that water can be frozen to create ice or heated to created steam, the energy simply takes different forms.

By the same rule money is simply energy, whether it's in the form of coins, notes, cheques, plastic cards, electronic transfers or computer print outs. It contains the same fundamental energy that is in you and the trees and the stars and in everything in our universe. Our whole world is energy in one form or another and that includes money.

Know that you can control energy so therefore you can control the money in your life. Energy never ceases to exist. It moves from one place to another and from one form to another so there is always a bountiful supply of energy available to you. To bring money into your life you need to bring energy into your life. You can do this by drawing it from nature, eating well and looking after your general health. You can draw it through a healthy spirituality, living from a place of goodwill and clearing out any old unfinished emotional baggage. You can draw it from your environment, clearing away clutter and creating a peaceful space and spending time in relaxation or meditation. Don't dwell on resentments or fears around money because these will block the financial energy around you.

Once you draw the energy to you it can then be converted into money. Focus on knowing that this can and will happen rather than trying to understand how. Trust that this is how the process works. Trust that there is enough money available for what you need to come to you. Get involved in the part of our world that involves money in any form that works for you. You have to have an involvement with money to allow the energy that you attract to you to transform into money.

Get active and stay confident. When you harness energy and involve yourself with a potential financial opportunity the money will start to pour in. Remember to let it flow in your life and know that more will follow.

Fear

When you open this book here it is because you are letting fear influence your experiences and your decisions. You may be very aware of this, feeling constantly worried about money or a particular financial situation, or you may not realise that fear is influencing you.

If you know what you are scared about, try to stop and think about the situation in a calm manner. Fear often leads to denial and avoidance and that will only make the matter worse. Get someone to talk the situation through with you. Don't panic and don't rush into quick-fix solutions that may only make matters worse in the long run.

When we are fearful we focus heavily on the future. We want to know everything that may happen and how it's all going to work out in the long run. Remember that you only need to know what is going to happen in the next three hours or three days, not more than that. By then something may have shifted in a way that you can't foresee now.

When we are fearful we lose sight of the fact that the universe is abundant and will provide for us as long as we make the effort ourselves to harness that abundance.

Remember that fear is a feeling. It's about anticipating the future negatively. As what you focus on grows, your fear will draw to you the impending negativity that you anticipate. You don't need to be afraid. You never get more than you can handle or deal with in each present moment of your experience. Dreading something is always more awful than actually experiencing it. Face your fears and you will be able to solve the financial issues in your life.

It may be that fear doesn't seem to be the problem. Instead your focus is on something else or someone else. But this is one of the ways that we avoid acknowledging our fears. We take the feelings and attach them to something completely unrelated. It's time to admit that you are worried about money, since with that admission comes the knowledge that you are worried about your own safety and security in the world, as this is what money represents. Get your money affairs in order, but also look at how you can make yourself feel properly safe and secure in other areas of your life.

Money can't chase your fears away, befriend them and then you'll be free of them.

Patience

When you open this book here, it is asking you to be patient about your financial situation. It is time to calmly accept that you cannot have exactly what you want or shift things in the way you would like right now and that you will have to wait before things will be seen to change.

Are you currently impatient with your financial situation or with someone involved in your finances? Or is it yourself you are impatient with? Is money not coming into your life at the speed or in the quantity that you desire? Maybe someone owes you some money and is slow or reluctant to pay you back. Are cheques getting stuck in the post or is a commission or deal you've been hoping for being delayed or cancelled?

Patience is an art form. It teaches us discipline and humility. It reminds us that we are not in charge of everything or everybody. Sometimes things unfold at a pace that isn't our pace. Maybe the universe wants you to slow down. Maybe it knows what is best for you more than you do. If everything goes according to your timing you may just find that you miss a wonderful opportunity which has only arisen from these apparently frustrating circumstances.

Patience is about perseverance. It's about sticking to your beliefs or to consistent action when the evidence that this works has not yet presented itself.

Look at the useful lesson that something like this can provide for you. If you had what you wanted now, what wouldn't you have to deal with? What challenges could be avoided? This is a brilliant opportunity for facing delay with equanimity. What will you do in the interim? How will you manage? Where will you put your focus? How deeply are you willing to trust in the future? Are you ready to believe that there will be a positive outcome in the long run?

Pay attention to your moods. Notice how you practise patience. Are you wound up like a coiled spring or are you able to properly relax and live with the period of waiting? How tolerant and understanding are you? How selfish and disagreeable can you be? Explore your frustration at not being able to control things as you would like.

Patience is about waiting, trusting, knowing and believing. Patience is about how powerfully you believe that the universe supports you. It goes against the flow of modern culture where all is scheduled and timetabled. It puts us back on our instincts and our intuition.

Let go of trying to control the outcome. Be patient.

Clarity

When you open this book here, it is telling you that the recipe for financial success and peace of mind is to be clear. This means that right now you need to know where you stand financially.

Get organised. Know your exact income and all of your expenditures. Buy a new book and start writing down everything that you need to spend money on. Separate the regular expenses from the more unpredictable ones and make sure that you do predict them. You need to keep a record of everything that you spend. If you don't know what is going on around your money then how can you steer it in the desired direction? Avoiding knowing simply fogs up the picture and makes money impossible to control.

Things need to be clear enough that nothing is obscured and nothing is hidden. How do you store your information? Make sure that everything is filed in an easy and accessible way that works for you. A good test is whether a stranger could easily find their way around your finances. If they couldn't, you're not being clear enough.

We also need clarity in our goals. What exactly do you want financially? Are you actually clear about how much money you have, how much money you want and what you want to do with your money?

Remember that money doesn't operate in isolation. It's a reflection of your self-worth and perceived value. You not only have to focus on financial clarity, you need to bring clarity into your life as a whole. Get practical. Switch off the TV for a week each month, clear out and clean out all of your clutter. Simplify your life. Work out what's getting in your way and deal with it. Spend some time in self reflection. Eat healthily, get fresh air regularly. As money is energy, you have to be clear about how much energy you are willing to expend towards your goals. How willing are you to improve the quality of your own energy? When you do you will be able to literally pull money into your life but it requires clarity.

When you open the book here, it can also mean that you are not stating your position clearly on something related to your money. Have you borrowed or lent money without being clear how it is to be returned? Are you taking on payments without being clear how you are going to meet them? Are you supported by, or supporting, someone else in a way that is not healthy? Make sure your financial transactions are 'clean' ones. When you buy things of dubious origin or fudge your accounts, even just to yourself, know that this has an unforeseen cost attached.

Clarity initially involves effort and honest behaviour but when you reap the rewards you'll know that it was worth it.

Blame

When you open this book here, it is because you are blaming money for what is going on in your life. You are reasoning that things are as they are solely because of your finances.

Blaming is all about refusing to take responsibility for yourself. It's about excuses and avoidance. What are you not doing because you feel that money won't allow it? Do you know that there are always ways around each situation if you are determined and committed enough? How many times recently have you talked of wanting to do something but not being able to afford it? Have you fully investigated what it would really cost? Have you looked at the cheaper options or the creative solutions that would allow you the freedom to proceed within your budget? If you couldn't blame it on the money what would you be free to do? You don't need a computer before you can write your book, you don't need huge savings before you can marry or leave your partner. You don't need to save enough to give up work before you can get involved in a new career. When you insist that you do, you are literally using money as an excuse to hold yourself back. It isn't your fault, it's the money. Or perhaps you have plenty of money and are blaming your problems on this.

Now is the time to stop pretending that money prevents you from living your life to the full. People have accomplished great things without letting money stand in their way. What could you organise right now? Can you exchange skills or services instead of paying for them? You can transform a home with a bit of imagination and fresh paint, you don't have to wait until you can afford to move. You can exercise at home without having to join a gym, you can join the library or adult education classes for anything that you want to know or learn.

Blame is about playing victim. It's about making money culpable for your life choices, rather than admitting that you are in charge of the money. If you don't have enough, go and earn some more or spend less. If you can't have everything that you want right now, then accept it and work out what your priorities are. If you've got lots of money then enjoy it, you don't need to make it into another problem. There's no benefit in complaining.

Giving away your power doesn't benefit anyone, especially you. When we stop blaming life or money then we reclaim our power. Then and only then are we are free to change our circumstances or adapt to them in a constructive way.

Blame breeds passivity. Get active instead and you are free to realise your true potential.

Creativity

When you open this book here, it is time to focus upon your creativity. It may be that you are feeling particularly creative and expressive right now and this is to reassure you that you are on the right path and that financial success will result as long as you bring your ideas to fruition.

It may be that you need to be creative about how you make your money. Or it may be about what you do with your money and how you spend it. Creativity can involve risk taking and as long as you act with care and self-respect, now is the time to go for what you want.

If your creativity has been ignored or discredited in the past or you are not aware of creativity as an issue in your life at the moment, now is the time to start exploring this. Creativity is not only the territory of the genius, the less academic or those with time on their hands. We all have it in us to be creative. Creativity is really about choosing how we do things and finding our own way, from inside us rather than from the outside world.

For when we tap into our true creativity we connect with our most powerful energy which then can be translated into financial success. Riches come from daring to really go within and bring what is there out into your life.

When we go within we can connect with all the wisdom and knowledge that we have collected throughout our lives. We also tap into the sea of eternal knowledge that floats forever around us in the universal energy. When ideas seem ahead of their time it is primarily because this art of connecting with the greater universal body of knowledge has been mastered so effectively. Many ideas and possibilities are much closer to you than you may think. Take time out to go within and access all of these floating ideas and possibilities. Because you are unique you will put your own individual spin on them and make them your own. You will enrich the world by bringing these ideas and possibilities into a physical form. In turn you will be enriched both by the joy of creativity and by the financial rewards it will draw to you.

When you believe in what you create you will find people who are willing to pay for your creations.

Trust yourself and be brave. You can do it.

Addiction

W hen you open this book here, it is a warning that you are using money addictively or that addictive behaviour is damaging your financial situation.

When you are driven by a compulsion that your willpower or common sense are unable to diffuse then you are addicted. Perhaps you are kidding yourself, insisting that you could stop whatever it is if you wanted to, but you are not demonstrating this through your behaviour. You aren't stopping and what you do, not what you say, is the measure of the truth.

Addictive behaviour comes about as an alternative to having our feelings. We do whatever the addictive behaviour is, to avoid or placate the part of us that doesn't feel OK. Mostly we go into the addictive behaviour so quickly, we don't even know that we had a feeling that we wanted to avoid. Alternatively we may be very aware of the unwelcome feeling and make a conscious decision to engage in the addictive, distracting behaviour to make ourselves feel better.

The key to breaking your addiction is to have the feelings you are so strongly avoiding and break the denial. Stop making excuses and get honest. Start to write down how you spend your money. What proportion is going on alcohol, junk food and impulse or comfort spending and how are these behaviours impacting on your earnings? How much do you spend on others to buy their love?

Look at your attitude to material possessions. Are they a choice or a need? A huge part of the population is constantly in debt because of our culture of addictive spending. Do you really need it that badly and if so, why? The availability of credit has made the situation all the worse.

It may also be that your addictive behaviour is standing in the way of future wealth, health and happiness. Are you being passed over for promotion because you spend too long in the pub or arrive at work with a hangover? Do you have low energy and low self-esteem from all the unhealthy food that you are spending your money on? Remember you need healthy, strong energy to attract the energy of wealth.

Mostly addictive spenders get the buzz out of the purchasing rather than ownership. A way to begin to break addictive spending is to take your purchases back to the store for a refund and begin to face that it is the shopping which comforts you rather than a real need of the goods.

If you know that your spending is really out of hand contact Debtors Anonymous, get advice from a debtors support group or see a counsellor or therapist. Now is the time to get the help you deserve.

Addiction is a lifelong challenge, but healing begins with taking one step after another and sticking at it. You can do it.

Stability

W hen you open this book here, it is encouraging you to explore the issue of stability in relation to your life generally and to your financial situation specifically.

Stability is all about keeping things balanced, where the forces having an influence on a situation are sufficiently equal to cancel each other out. Thus when we are financially stable we are spending but we are also earning. We are dealing with today but we are also making provisions for tomorrow. Is this how you are acting or are you out of balance? Address it now.

You need to look at what forces and influences you are creating in your life financially and how they stack up as whole. Are you overstretching yourself? If so, what factors exist to balance this situation? If you are waiting for a guaranteed inheritance or payment from a reliable source it is different to hoping that everything will magically level out or praying to win the lottery.

By their very nature, extremes are not stable. The whole basis of the playground seesaw rests on the fact that it is far easier to tip the balance the other way when one is furthest from the centre. This is true financially. People who live modestly while avoiding risk have fewer surprises in their lives while those who take risks have to be prepared to fall far, when they do fall. Check where you are on this scale and shift yourself further towards the centre. If you are terribly cautious you need to open up a little without becoming reckless. If you are very confident about taking risks perhaps it's time to take a closer look at the financial burdens that you have taken on, or are about to take on, and think about your situation more carefully.

When we are dealing with money we need to realise that all life and all energy pulsates, it regularly expands and contracts, closes and opens. This is its essential nature and we need to learn to pulsate with it. It's important not to get stuck in either being too open or too closed around money. Sometimes you have to let money flow out but know when to stem the flow. Other times you can get too caught up in savings or restricting your spending too much and become so closed that money cannot flow towards you. Then you need to begin to open up, spend a little, let go a little, so that the energy and thus the money can flow freely.

The tides will turn and you must turn with them without being too extreme. This is the nature of life and money. Listen to the voice in your head more carefully, tune into to your instincts more often, and create stability in your life now.

Spirituality

When you open this book here let your mind be at peace. It is time to understand the link between spirituality and money, and to know that there is a place for both in your life. It is all about balance.

Are you struggling to find a way to be spiritual while having money or to have money while being spiritual? Some of us are taught to believe that these two cannot go hand in hand. That to be truly spiritual you must be poor or that if you are rich you cannot be spiritual.

Neither of these is true. It is totally possible to have lots of money and at the same time having a deep and satisfying spirituality.

The key is to understand that each can have its place in your life, without it taking over. Money is important, but it isn't everything. It can make life more pleasant, but by itself it cannot bring you lasting joy. Don't prioritise money too highly.

Spirituality is important too. A life led without any spiritual dimension, where materialism is too important, is an empty one in which the heart and the soul are pushed to one side. But don't force yourself to go without and think that this will develop your spirituality. Going without makes us uncomfortable and needy which isn't the right environment for spiritual growth. Use your money to be kind to yourself and create the right context for your spirituality to flourish.

Whatever your spiritual beliefs are, what matters is that you find them for yourself and hold them close to you, without condemning others who hold different beliefs. When you trust in a force greater than yourself then you will know that you are not alone with this issue. Ask for support and guidance and trust where this takes you.

Through spiritual beliefs you can understand and celebrate the meaning of life. With money you can take pleasure in your life. Let generosity be the glue that holds these two together. Give with a good heart, of your money and your spirituality, and you will never be without either.

Boundaries

W hen you open this book here, you need to explore your boundaries and how these impact on your financial position. Boundaries mark where things begin and end, they make issues specific rather than vague.

Good boundaries are clearly visible and firmly positioned. They are not easily dislodged or uprooted. For example we mark our garden with a fence and anticipate that people will understand that this is the line that they should not cross without permission. Such a boundary is very physical but we must also have boundaries around our possessions, our behaviour and ourselves. Some boundaries are cultural, some are learnt within the family and society and some we simply create ourselves.

What are your boundaries around money? What are your limits? How do you specify and set limits upon what is yours and not yours? Do you loan money without limits, failing to agree when it will be returned? Do you let people steal objects or money from you without really acknowledging it as theft? Do you let another dip into your purse or bank account because you haven't set a clear enough boundary around what is yours and not theirs?

Often we have a boundary but have no sense of how to hold it when it is threatened. Then it becomes the same as not having one. To hold a boundary we have to get clear and consistent. We have to let people know about our boundaries and be willing to take action if they do not respect them. You have power in this situation. Change bank accounts, don't lend someone money the next time, keep your purse with you in future. You can work out a solution.

Boundaries are about self-control and self-respect. They are also about respecting others. Whose boundaries are you breaking or attempting to invade? It's easy to push others and manipulate them into giving us what we want but know that when you do this it is always at a price. Resentment and anger are the most likely outcome even when they are not immediately obvious.

You may need to look at how you fail to set or respect boundaries with yourself. What are your limits financially? Do you spend too much on others or on yourself? Do you make promises with yourself that you don't keep? Having and keeping to your own boundaries takes commitment and discipline. It's about restricting yourself appropriately. Now is the time to do this.

Go ahead and discover how wonderful it feels to be in charge of yourself rather than at the mercy of your own ego.

Rejection

When you open this book here, it is time to recognise that currently you are not having a healthy or mature relationship with money. You are holding yourself away from it because you have developed the belief that it is not for you.

Maybe money was seen as dirty or shameful in your family of origin or you just believe that you'll never be lucky enough to have it. Are you relying on someone else to help you out, to pay your bills or to loan you money or are you spending too much on others and leaving too little for yourself? We can't totally reject money and survive in the world today. To rely on others to deal with money for us so that we can avoid it and so avoid resolving our relationship with it is neither fair nor honest. It's time to grow up; it's time to change.

Know that there is nothing wrong with having more than enough money to satisfy your needs. Money is clean and pure. There is no reason to reject it. You are in the world at this time to have a proper relationship with money, for this is one of the challenges and lessons of being human in this lifetime. Don't avoid it or it will come back at you.

If you feel that showing an interest in money reflects badly on you, know that you are mistaken. Much good can be accomplished when we have enough money both for ourselves and for others. While selfish, irresponsible materialism isn't good for anyone, it isn't the money that is to blame here; it's how it is used.

By contrast you may be rejecting money not because you think that money itself is bad but because you think that to reject money is good. There is a strong movement in the world which links either poverty or extreme generosity to spirituality but this is only true for the tiny minority, who are almost finished with the physical world. By rejecting money you are not making yourself more spiritual. Rather you are avoiding the lesson of how to be spiritual in a material and physical world. If you didn't need this lesson you would be a spirit right now rather than a human. Know that part of being human is to manage to develop a healthy relationship with money. You need to be able to provide for yourself and enjoy the benefits of your own money.

Money is simply the physical manifestation of our energy, in a form that we all agree upon. It represents the exchange of goods or services between one person and another. Don't reject it or throw it away. Allow it to be your friend.

Loving

When you open this book here, it is to remind and focus you upon the potentially loving nature of your money. How we behave with our money tells us a lot about how we treat others and ourselves.

How loving are you being right now? Are you treating yourself with love and respect in the way that you gather, use and manage your money? Are you treating others in a loving way too?

Remember that you are only loving when you act from your heart with honourable intentions. To attempt to buy someone's love or control others is not loving behaviour. If this is what you are doing, face it honestly and be willing to stop.

When you are loving in a financial way, it is important to get the balance right. Are you giving too much to another and not looking after your own needs sufficiently? If so you are failing to be loving towards yourself. Or are you too concerned with being loving towards yourself and neglecting those around you with adverse results? It's time for change.

You also need to recognise the importance of tough loving around money. To overindulge yourself and call it love is dishonest and unhealthy. You need to moderate yourself and find your equilibrium. The same is true in relation to others. Are you really being loving by taking on the level of financial responsibility that you do? Should you be doing more or should you be doing less? Often stepping back and letting others fend for themselves is the hardest but the most honest loving act that we can offer. Recognise what is really required of you rather than avoiding your part or throwing money at a situation and calling it love. If you are ungenerous with others learn to let go and let your love manifest in a positive, tangible way.

Loving is about the nurturing aspects of money. Be kind to yourself and to those that you love. But don't let it stop there. Learn to expand your experience of loving to include those that you don't know personally. The huge array of charities that abound nowadays may leave you feeling overwhelmed and detached but don't let this be an excuse to withhold your loving contribution. Pick any cause that appeals to you and contribute regularly. It's your opportunity to be financially loving.

Use money to love yourself, love others and spread love in the world. It will bring you enormous pleasure.

Interference

When you open this book here, it is because there is an outside force intervening in your financial situation that is not beneficial to you.

Perhaps you are receiving advice from others that you haven't actually asked for, or maybe you asked for limited support and now you feel that they have moved in and taken over. Or have you become financially entangled with another person? Money is a difficult and sensitive subject. Sometimes it's hard to establish how much outside involvement is helpful and it's hard to judge the quality of the advice you get. But interference means that you have definitely passed the threshold of what is useful and appropriate.

It's time to draw back. It's time to assert yourself and clarify that your finances are your own business. Other people may have strong opinions about how you manage them but ultimately it is your choice and your responsibility.

Check that you are truly responsible for yourself financially. It is so easy to be financially entangled with partners, family or friends and then to not feel free or able to make your own financial decisions. Get clear as to which money is yours, whether it is a salary, an inheritance or an allowance. Then make sure that those around you know that what you do with your money is up to you. Obviously if there are shared financial responsibilities these must be agreed and paid for but you should always have some money that is totally your own, no matter how little this is.

Review your arrangement if you are financially dependent on another. It is always best to be financially independent as this gives you the greatest potential to truly be yourself. Relying on another invariably leads to resentment on both sides and to one person feeling controlled and the other feeling drained. The person providing the money ends up feeling that they have the right to decide how the money is spent.

If you have young children and only one partner is earning then get really clear that this is what you both want and that both of you are working in different ways to bring in this single salary. Share the money equally as soon as you get it and this will reduce negative interference.

If you are the person interfering in someone else's finances then now is the time to separate. Let the other person be responsible for themselves and stop trying to control them. Recognise how great your investment is in being the provider or advisor and then let it go. Find the pleasure in letting your relationship be more equal.

Untangle yourself financially from those around you and watch your abilities around money grow.

Live in the Present

L iving in the present is the basis of all the great Eastern religions and philosophies. Yet in modern society the past and the future dominate. We base our expectations of the future on our experiences in the past. For example we judge something to be a good investment because of how it performed before. The money markets and the economy all rely on predicting the future based on the past.

We do the same in our own lives. We put a lot of energy into remembering the past and planning for the future, when in truth we only exist in the present. Our power lies in the present moment. If we want to do anything, feel anything, change anything then we can only do it now.

What is actually happening in your life, right now, at this moment? Do you need to do something differently? Are you regretting something that you did in the past? Are you worrying about the future when in fact today things are OK? Or are you piling up financial worries that may well be resolved long before you actually get to them? It's time to stop.

Having your brain go over and over the details of the past or the future is a habit that you have developed and that you can break. Make the decision that just for today you will only focus on today. This doesn't mean neglecting your responsibilities but it does mean being willing to accept who you are and how your life is today. Pay today's bills, make today's financial decisions. Be satisfied, generous and trusting. Or if things are tough be nice to yourself and know that tomorrow is another day.

Living in the present means being with yourself and as such it is the biggest gift that you can ever give yourself.

Relax, breathe, be calm and keep everything as simple as possible. Enjoy today and each day, one day at a time. Know that living in the present will stabilise you financially and that good things will be your reward.

Denial

When you open this book here, it is because you are failing to recognise how much of an issue money is in your life. Perhaps you are already hearing this from those close to you or perhaps it is a complete surprise. But if you are willing to accept the truth in this then you will soon begin to recognise that the evidence is all around you.

What is your relationship with money? Has it always caused you problems or is this a new phase in your life? Be honest. Are your debts bigger than you can comfortably manage, do you limp from one pay cheque to another or are you permanently overdrawn? Have you got yourself into a financial commitment that is too big for you or with someone who isn't sufficiently trustworthy? Alternatively do you actually have plenty of money and refuse to let yourself accept and enjoy it or do you live a life that doesn't fulfil you in order to have the money it provides? Whatever it is, you are denying the extent of the problems it is creating for you.

The trouble with denial is that you will be working really hard not to face it, which means that you may continue to do this even as you read about your denial here. Know that the choice is yours. You can stay in denial for as long as you like but it will have consequences. The longer you stay in denial the more time you will waste without being able to enjoy your money or the bigger the mess you will be left with when you are finally forced to admit that there is a problem.

It can seem easier to bury your head in the sand than deal with your money issues right now, but it is not. Your avoidance is costing you dearly, both financially and emotionally. Ironically dealing with it would actually feel much better than you realise. It would bring enormous relief and you could start afresh with greater awareness and honesty. Help is around you. Ask people you trust for advice. There are many agencies available to support those in financial difficulties and if you have money that you can't enjoy you can get help to encourage you to let yourself spend some of it.

Don't feel ashamed or embarrassed to admit that there is a problem. Be proud of yourself. You are brave to come out of denial. Even though it may take some time to sort out your current issues, the sooner you begin, the sooner you will be free of them.

Accept and deal with the reality of your present situation and you empower yourself for the future.

Fudging the Truth

W hen you open this book here it asks you to confront the issue of fudging the truth around money in your life.

When you say one thing while doing another you are fudging. When you pretend that things are fine when actually they are not, you are fudging. When you hide the truth from others or from yourself you are fudging. The trouble with fudging is that things never work out in the long term as you'd hoped. It generates a sense of discomfort and it destroys trust. The gap between what you say and what you do eventually comes back to haunt you.

We all have the ability to fudge the truth, to hide or push uncomfortable facts aside and settle for a pleasant fantasy. Facing this part of yourself takes bravery, because it means facing the ways in which you manipulate the truth, avoid responsibility and gloss over painful realities. It also means that you might have to make changes in the way you're behaving.

To face this and to take control of it is to take responsibility for your behaviour in the most positive way. Begin by being honest about the ways in which you fudge. Do you pretend to have more in the bank than you really have or to earn more? Do you tell yourself you can afford the thing you want when actually you can't? Do you use cheques and credit cards to avoid being honest about what you can afford?

If so then it's time to get straight and clear around money. Learning how to manage your money well is vital if you want to increase the amount of money you have, to draw abundance in your life or to be successful in a financial venture. Be honest about what you have and what you spend. Keep accounts and make a spending plan which is realistic, then stick to it.

If it is someone else who is fudging the truth around money in your life know that you've attracted them because this is what you are doing too. When you change, this will change.

Straightening out your fudging will help you to get clear about the amount of money you really need. Once you are meeting your financial needs appropriately and are in control of your spending then, and only then, can you begin to attract enough money into your life to play with and to make your wishes come true.

When you stop fudging you'll feel a huge sense of relief and you'll quickly see the rewards that this will bring.

Freedom

When you open this book here it is because you need to separate yourself from the opinions of the masses. You are automatically following, without question, the huge number of established beliefs and rituals around money that the modern world feeds you. But it is time to establish your own beliefs and opinions about money rather than accepting those of your culture as the only reality.

Every society requires that you abide by a number of laws and rules to stay within the law. But you can do this and still have your own rules and behaviours around your money. You can be legal and unconventional.

Question your habits. Do you spend money you can ill afford on gifts, guests or holidays because that's what those around you do or expect of you? Have a go at changing what you do. Spend a penny where you'd be expected to spend a pound and vice versa. Prove to yourself that what you spend is your own choice.

Or perhaps you moderate your spending too much when you can well afford what you want, because you're worried about what others will think of you enjoying your wealth. Set yourself free. You can do it your way now, rather than looking for approval.

It's time to liberate yourself. It's time to take responsibility for all of your financial actions including the choices you make, no matter how unconventional these are. Behave decently and responsibly but do what works for you rather than what's expected. Do your own thing because freedom brings with it the opportunity to excel financially.

Recognise how many set expectations you have around money and release yourself from them. How much do you think anyone can earn in an hour, a day or a lifetime? Know that this is only limited when you tie yourself into mass thinking. Anyone can be paid ten times the going rate if they are brave enough to charge that much and willing to put the work into finding the person who will pay it. Remember that anything's possible when you set yourself free.

You can be richer and freer than you ever dreamed of or happy to live on far less than you ever imagined if you are willing to break out of society's expectations of you. Work out what's right for you. Where would you be financially if there were no rules about how much money you could live on, want, have, earn or win?

Know that there are no rules. You are already free. You can stand outside of the crowd anytime that you want. Do it now.

Saving

There is no quicker way to riches than to involve yourself in saving money because the moment that you have some money put aside you have abundance and abundance always attracts greater abundance.

You can save in two ways. You can save something for the future, so that it is there for you when you want it at a later date. Or you can look for bargains and save by spending less on necessities or luxuries than you expected. You opened this book here because you need to look at both of these issues in relation to your finances.

Saving is healthy, mature behaviour around money as long as it is done in a moderate, balanced manner. There is no point saving like mad for the future and living a life of poverty in the present unless you have a clear goal and objective that makes the lean times worthwhile. Just as it's also unwise to spend all you have today and run up debts without saving any money for the future or for unseen difficulties. A rule of thumb is to save 5 to 12 per cent of your income. Put it somewhere that you can't access it easily and don't spend it at the first opportunity. Think about two savings accounts. One for short-term goals and another for the long term. Once long-term savings have grown a little it is then wise to invest them so that they grow more efficiently. Get financial advice for this.

If saving is something that you have always rejected then start small but do start now. There is a great deal of satisfaction in watching your money grow. Also work on clearing your debts too because then spare cash can go to your savings rather than servicing your debt.

At the same time you need to address where you could be spending less of your money for the same end result. Start shopping around. Check prices and notice where you can get the same goods or equivalent ones cheaper. Follow the old saying that when you look after the pennies the pounds will look after themselves. But don't get so focused on saving that you become tight or mean because this will undermine the flow of money towards you and keep you focused on the future rather than enjoying living in the present. Make sure to control the way you let your money leave you. You should let your money go through choice rather than ignorance or neglect. As you let it go bless it and appreciate it and then it will return to you at a later date.

Enjoy saving and avoid waste, while still allowing yourself frivolity and you'll find that managing your money will be so much easier.

Abundance

When you open this book here it is time to be happy, relax and trust that all will be well, because abundance is coming into your life.

Financial abundance means having enough money to take care of all your needs and yet still having plenty over with which to enjoy yourself and bring yourself and others pleasure.

We all have the ability to attract abundance to us. You have the potential to act like a magnetic force that will pull wealth towards you. There is more than enough for everyone in the world, money is passed constantly from hand to hand and as it circulates you can choose to draw what you want and need to you.

In order to attract abundance you need to focus clearly on the amount of money you want and the path it will take into your life, such as earnings, winnings or a gift. Know what you want it for and what you will do with it and make sure that you put it all in writing and sign it.

Believe that there is enough for all and that you are entitled to your share. Trust that it is coming and feel yourself drawing it towards you. Money likes money. It flows towards a sense of abundance and richness. When we genuinely feel rich the money out there feels it too and is drawn by a gravitational pull to seek us out. So if you feel rich stick with it. If you don't feel rich then start to make sure that you have a bit of spare cash put aside, no matter how small and let yourself feel rich because of this.

If you are out of balance financially realise that you are in a vicious circle. When you are abundant from a place of debt you push true abundance further away. Only when you admit that this is what you are doing will you be free to stop debting.

It is important also to believe that you deserve abundance and to know how to handle it, otherwise you may quickly lose it when you find it. Many have drawn money to themselves, only to spend, gamble or give it away because they feel uncomfortable or guilty having it.

Remember, the more money you have, the more responsibilities you will inherit. Before abundance comes to you make sure that you are ready for it and that you truly want it. Be willing to be trustworthy and honest with your money and to share it with others responsibly.

Then sit back and enjoy your abundance because you deserve it.

Fun

When you open this book here it is a gift. The message waiting for you is that it is time to have fun and enjoy yourself and your money.

Making and managing money can be a very serious business. So much so that we often forget how important it is to enjoy the fruits of our labour. Of course it is important to pay for your food, housing and essential needs. But it is also important to set a little time and money aside for having fun.

Often as adults we forget how to have fun. We think we're not entitled to it, that only children have fun yet nothing could be further from the truth. Having fun is as important to our health and well-being as sleep and food. Fun means different things to each of us and it is for you to decide how you'd like to have fun. What makes you laugh, what have you always longed to do which would give you enormous pleasure, what makes you feel excited?

If you are faced with a difficulty or decision right now, go for the option that would make you feel happier in your heart. Is there something that you need to resolve before you can be free to have fun? Is there a way that you can resolve it in a light-hearted, fun manner? If it is at all possible take this approach.

Give yourself permission to use your money to bring fun into your life. This isn't about being irresponsible; it's about finding affordable ways to truly enjoy yourself. Get in touch with the child inside you that each of us has and find out what he or she wants. Then be willing to let them have it, no matter how silly it may seem to you.

Trust that this is the time for fun and it will lead you to a better place.

Independence

W hen you open this book here it asks you to think about how much you depend on others to provide or manage your money. Do you live on an income that someone else earns, even though you could earn money for yourself? Or do you leave it to others to take responsibility for organising and dealing with your money?

Perhaps you still rely on a parent, partner or friend to pay for you when you need extra money or want something that you can't afford. If so then it may be time to move on and claim your independence.

Depending inappropriately on others weakens our self-esteem and our ability to manage for ourselves. It deprives us of the opportunity to feel good about our money and the way we earn, manage and spend it.

Allowing another to pay for you can mean allowing them to control you. Do you feel you must go along with the wishes of the person who pays for you? Do you resent them? Then it is time to take a step towards independence and to claim for yourself the right to make your own decisions and manage for yourself. This may feel difficult. Perhaps you don't trust your own ability to make or manage money. But believe you have that ability and that you can use it if you choose to and then act on this belief. Do something about it, so that you can start to rely on yourself. Independence is vital to becoming a mature adult. Yet we must all interlink with and depend on others as well as stand on our own two feet.

You may be so fiercely independent that you won't take a penny if it is given to you and you push away others' help and generosity. If so then it is time to soften your outlook and accept the love of others, in the form of money and financial support.

The secret is to get the balance right. Depend too much on others and you topple over, too little and you become rigid. True independence brings confidence, self-esteem and freedom of choice. It's time to let yourself experience this.

Visualisation

When you open this book here it is time to use the power of your thoughts and imagination to attract money into your life and accomplish your goals. To visualise something is to make it visible in your mind and it is a powerful truth that what you first see in your mind is what becomes real in your life. Believe it and you will see it.

The power of our minds is enormous. Thoughts are like living beings that travel out from us and attract what we are thinking about into our lives. Yet so many people dismiss their thoughts as powerless, or think negative thoughts that only act to keep them stuck where they are. Do you tell yourself that you aren't lucky, that you won't get the pay rise you want or that you'll always struggle to find enough money? Be careful because if you think these things they will come true.

Visualisation is a wonderful way of creating new, positive thoughts and changing our old poverty-conscious beliefs into new abundance-filled ones.

Visualisation is very easy. Anyone can do it. Just picture in your mind whatever it is that you want and focus on that picture as often as you can. Remember to also clear out your negative images by releasing. Say aloud everyday 'I release the need to be broke' or in debt or whatever it is that fits for you. Then add affirmations such as 'I am lucky, I attract money to me' or 'I earn a great salary' to add strength to your vision. Create pictures in your mind of yourself changing and getting what you want.

A lovely way of visualising is the dream bubble. Cup your hand and see in your palm the scene that you want to draw to you. For instance picture yourself in the beautiful home you would like or the job you long for. Close your palm and pluck an imaginary golden thread from the air. Use it to sew the dream bubble closed, then, keeping one end of the thread between your thumb and forefinger open your hand and throw the dream bubble out into the universe. Then tuck the end of the golden thread into your belt or waistband and pat it three times. Do this every morning until your dream comes true.

Keep on visualising, make it part of your everyday life and you'll soon see what a vital financial tool it is.

Debt

When you open this book here it is because debt has become an issue in your life and it is holding you back.

In modern living owing money to others has come to be accepted as normal. Many people have mortgages, credit cards, hire purchase agreements and loans. But along with bringing the material goods that you want, debt can be a drain on your energy and a source of worry and unrest.

If you are considering taking on debt then ask yourself, is what I want worth the demands the debt will make on my time, my emotions and my energy? Sometimes it is better to wait for what you want and save for it first rather than rushing ahead to get something quickly and then paying for it later. Because when we take on debt we not only pay the interest on it we also pay emotionally for the burden of the debt.

How much of your income goes on paying debts? It is wise to keep your debts few and for particular purposes only. Avoid borrowing on a whim and spending money that you don't have just to comfort yourself or to make yourself feel better. By trying to borrow the most that we can at one time while making the minimum repayments on the debt we bury ourselves under the weight of our debts and we limit ourselves for the whole period we are repaying the loan. Instead think about the long-term consequences, not just about today. If you are trying to make a decision about something make an honest appraisal of what borrowing really costs you and be more realistic about your circumstances.

If you already have debts which are worrying you or beginning to feel out of control, get outside help and support in working out a plan to repay them in a way that you can manage. Call Debtors Anonymous and get hold of one of the many good books on getting out of debt. Debt can feel like a pool of thick mud, where your feet are stuck and it is impossible to take a step forward. But by facing your debts you can lift your feet free and step into the clear waters of debt-free living.

Debt can become a way of life and a way of holding yourself back. Freed from the burden of debt you can make new choices about the way you use your money and create new energy for yourself around your money. The power lies with you.

Choice

When you open this book here it is time to recognise the importance of choice in your life. Although it may not feel true at the moment, you need to know that you have a choice about the way you draw money to you and a choice about the way you use your money.

Choice means knowing that there are alternatives and selecting the one that suits you. In every situation there is always an alternative and yet we tend to be in the habit of thinking that things can only be the way they are.

Look again at the way you are around money. Do you earn or acquire it in the way you want to? Do you have what you need and desire and do you use money wisely and generously? If not then you can choose to begin, now.

Don't make a financial decision from a position in which you feel you have no choice. Investigate the options; get creative and think of other ways of doing it. Give yourself choices.

Perhaps you are feeling stuck, trapped or restricted by forces and conditions beyond your control. Perhaps you long to change your job, earn more or to spend your money in a different way but there seems to be no choice about the situation you are in.

As long as you believe that you have no choice this will be true. When you don't know that you have choices it's easy to believe that you are powerless and can be controlled by other people and events. In fact you are never powerless.

The situation you are in is the one you have chosen for yourself right now. If it is an uncomfortable or unhappy one, know that you chose it because there is a benefit to you in it somewhere. Recognise the benefit of this situation, whatever it is, and take responsibility for yourself and your circumstances. In this way you take the power for your life and your future back into your own hands. If you can see no way out of your situation know that you are simply unwilling to deal with the consequences of the choices you could make to get out of it. In this way you paralyse yourself. But you don't have to. Make a choice and deal with what it brings. As you do so a multitude of choices open up before you. At every step, in every area of your life, you have a choice. If you want change then you can bring it about.

With choice comes freedom. There are no limits to what you can do and be and what you can resolve around your financial circumstances.

Lessons

When you open this book here it is time to think about the lesson life is giving you around money right now, whether you have an excess or very little. Perhaps you are struggling financially or perhaps you've lost money in some way. Are you finding that the way you make money is making you unhappy, have you been cheated out of money recently or have you got yourself into debt?

Learning our lessons can be very hard, especially if it's a situation that we've been in before and find ourselves in again. If you've cleared your debts and then run them up again, if you've lost a job only to lose another, if you've been conned several times or some other painful experience has repeated itself then you may be feeling angry, anxious or afraid. You may feel that you have bad luck or that it's impossible for you to escape from unhappiness.

Take comfort in the knowledge that whatever is happening in your life now will pass. And remember that the universe will always give you what you need before it gives you what you want. If you need to learn a particular lesson it will come round again and again until you fully learn the lesson and can continue on your way, stronger and wiser.

Ask yourself what lesson it is that you have been given and what it is you have to gain from it. What is it you need to see or understand, in order to move on? Perhaps you need to value what you have, before you can have more, or to change the way you use or acquire money so that you are being honest and true to yourself. Maybe you won't resolve things until you follow your heart and do what you are truly meant to do.

Whatever the lesson is, accept it with courage and remember that the painful step you are taking now is a step along the path to peace of mind, abundance and fulfilment.

Beyond today's lesson is tomorrow's reward. Because once we have accepted and grown through the lessons we are given, our dreams will begin to come true.

Appreciation

When you open this book here it is time to appreciate all of the abundance that you have in your life. If things are going well, money is flowing towards you or something has turned out as you hoped it would, now is the time to rejoice. Let yourself feel the pleasure of this. Share your good fortune by telling those close to you. Celebrate. Be proud and know that the future looks bright.

Perhaps you've been feeling hard done by lately, or worrying that you won't be able to make ends meet. Do you feel you don't have enough money, or that there are too many financial pressures in your life? Focusing your thoughts on these things will only increase them, for whatever you hold in your mind is what will appear and grow in your life. Opening the book here means it is time to focus on the richness and plenty in your life, even if at first you feel there is very little. Look at the things around you that your money has bought, are you able to eat today and do you have a roof over your head? Think of the bills you are able to pay, the pleasures money brings to your life even if it's only in small ways. Give thanks for all these things and fill your heart with appreciation for the source of your income and for your ability to earn or attract it.

Appreciate the gifts you are given and the abundance that comes your way, both small and large. Perhaps someone buys you a drink or you find a coin in the street. Don't dismiss these things. Accept that you deserve them and more will come your way. If there is something which you need to deal with around money appreciate the fact that you have the ability to do what needs doing. Appreciate the choices in your life and then go ahead and put them into practice.

Never take money for granted. The universe gives to those who value what they have and take care of it. Don't throw away what can still be used. Give it to a charity shop, a second-hand sale or to someone who will in turn appreciate it.

Appreciation means treating money and all that it brings you with love and respect. As you begin to do this the value of what you have will grow and you will attract greater abundance to you.

Trust

When you open this book here it is time to look at the issue of trust around your money. To trust is to have faith that the decision or outcome will be for the best or that someone will do what they say they will. Trust requires honesty and integrity both in yourself and in people that you deal with. It's about believing that all will be as it should be. The universe knows what you need.

Perhaps you need to address a lack of trust. Do you trust that there will be enough money in your life for all your needs or are you afraid that someone will let you down around money? It's important to check out anything or anyone that you don't trust. Look carefully at your doubts and ask questions.

Trust begins with your own instincts. Trust yourself to know who will treat you and your money fairly and decently and let go of those who won't. Take your time in deciding who to trust. Look at their behaviour. Is it straight, honest, clear and reliable? If you're involved with someone that you don't trust around money then look at your own behaviour and be honest about where you are less than trustworthy too. For whatever you see in another will be a reflection of yourself. When you become more trustworthy around money you'll find yourself dealing with others who are more trustworthy too.

If you don't trust yourself or your ability to earn or keep money then start to turn this around. Look at all that you do in your life where you are trustworthy. Believe that you can handle money in the same way. The more you trust yourself the more trustworthy you will be. Make agreements with yourself and stick to them. Appreciate yourself for being trustworthy and for learning to trust. Most important of all trust the universe to give you what you need and what you want. Trust that there is enough for all and that you have the ability to attract your share.

Be prepared to work and put energy into drawing money to you and trust that it will come at exactly the right time.

Receive

When you open this book here you can be glad, as it is time to allow yourself to receive money and the good things which money can bring.

We often imagine it is easier to give than to receive, but for many of us this isn't so. Giving to others is often much easier than giving to ourselves or accepting the generosity of others.

Do you put all kinds of obstacles in the way of letting yourself receive? Do you find it hard to thank people who give to you? Do you insist that you will never have good fortune, that winning the lottery or making money is for others? Do you push abundance away from you, spending money as fast as it comes in just so that you won't have the discomfort of having it? If so you need to learn how to receive in a way that will give you pleasure and attract more abundance into your life. You need to be willing to take steps and make choices that allow money and what it buys into your life.

When we don't know how to receive good things we often won't let them into our lives and we are destructive, grumpy, depressed or ill if they do come our way. Or we accept them and then believe we have to return double what we received to compensate. This is because we feel we don't deserve to receive them. The picture we have of ourselves on the inside, which is unworthy, undeserving and unlovable doesn't match the outside picture of a person who deserves good fortune. In order to receive with pleasure and appreciation we need to make the inner and outer pictures match. This means raising your self-esteem so that you feel deserving and lovable on the inside.

Begin by giving to yourself. Give yourself small pleasures and gifts. Let yourself enjoy them and feel good about having them. The more you practise this the more easily it will come to you.

Stop putting obstacles in your path which ensure that you can't have what you want. Willingly embrace whatever you are given, no matter how large or small. Let yourself accept it with warmth and appreciation. Let the joy of receiving into your heart. As you learn to accept gifts, abundance and strokes of good fortune into your life you will attract more of them.

Let Go

When you open this book here it is time to let go of something or someone in your life connected with money. Who or what are you hanging on to which no longer gives you any true benefit? Is it or are they keeping you stuck or draining your energy and resources? Or are you trying to control something that isn't yours to control? Let go, for it has run its natural course.

Perhaps it is time to move on from your job. Is it making you unhappy or frustrated? Is there something you'd much rather do but which you're afraid may make you less money or provide less status? It may feel like a leap into the unknown, away from the familiar and comfortable. But if you don't take it you'll never know the happiness and fulfilment that are waiting for you when you do what is truly right for you.

If you make your money by doing a job that you dislike you will not be able to genuinely value yourself or what you earn. Make your money by doing work you like and respect and you will attract all the money you need. And you may well find that you need a lot less once you are content.

Perhaps you need to let go of someone who handles money for

you, or advises you? Or to let go of someone you work with or plan to work with. Perhaps you need to leave someone that you are financially dependent on. Have the courage to say no to people who don't have your best interests at heart, or when it no longer works for you.

Do you need to let go of debt? Some of us become so attached to owing money that, despite wishing to be debt-free we hang on to our debts no matter what. If this is you then be really honest with yourself. Decide how to clear your debts and stick to the plan you have made. Tell yourself that you are worth the effort. Allow yourself the pleasure of being in credit and staying there. Once you make the decision to let go of your debts and follow through by starting to pay them off, help and support will come your way. You will pay off your debts faster than you imagined possible.

Letting go is an act of faith. Until you let go of something you no longer need or want there will be no space for something new and exciting to come into your life.

Close a door so that another may open.

Confidence

When you open this book here be joyful. It is time to let yourself be bold, brave and trusting around money.

Having confidence means believing in yourself, trusting yourself and your judgement and being willing to rely on yourself and make decisions without always deferring to others.

Confidence is a quality that is self-perpetuating. The more you have, the more you gain, because confidence brings success and success brings more confidence. Allow yourself to believe in yourself.

Has your confidence in money matters been low? Do you rely on others, afraid to handle things yourself? Do you always take the timid approach, without any risks or surprises? Do you tell yourself you're playing it safe, when actually you don't have the confidence to do it any other way?

Confidence is very different to brashness, boasting and having loud opinions. Behaviours like these are simply to cover up a lack of confidence. True confidence is quiet, calm and trustworthy. It involves care, thought and a gut feeling about what is right in any given situation.

If your confidence around money is low then you can build it up for yourself. Be willing to trust yourself and make your own decisions. Listen to your inner voice, the part of you that has good judgement and is wise. Look at any successes you have had with money in the past, however small, and use the skills that worked then. Praise yourself for the things you do well, while forgiving yourself for mistakes. Learn the difference between a foolish risk and a well-judged one. Create a strategy for dealing with your money. Get help if you need it but don't blindly assume that others know best. Have the confidence to trust that you can guide yourself on to the right path.

Nurture your confidence and see it blossom. It will bring you precious rewards.

Beliefs

You have opened this book here because some of your beliefs are holding you back financially, and you need to find out what they are and change them.

Most of our beliefs about the world and ourselves begin when we are small children and alter very little as we grow up. Very often we aren't even aware that these are our beliefs, we think that they are simply reality. Yet they are the basis of how we function in the world. All our thoughts and actions are based on our deeply held and often unconscious beliefs. They rule our lives.

It is time to look at your beliefs around money. Write a list of all your beliefs starting each one with either 'I should', 'I shouldn't', 'I can't', 'I must', 'Money is', or 'Money isn't'.

Do you believe you are not entitled to have money, or that you can't have more than anyone else in your family? Do you believe money is scarce, hard to come by, evil or dirty? Do you believe that to be poor is safer or more worthy than being rich? Beliefs like these will lead you to avoid situations that might bring money to you. Or they can lead you to reject money when you could have it, or to give it away when you do get it. It's time to stop letting old beliefs control you but first you need to find out what they are.

Look through your list and practise saying 'I release the need to . . .' finishing with the belief that you don't want. Think about the beliefs you would like to have. For instance 'I attract money to me and I know how to use it responsibly and well.' 'I am entitled to be well-paid for what I do.' 'Money is valuable and can do a great deal of good.' Write them down and say them aloud. Stick them up on your wall and look at them everyday.

Changing long-held beliefs doesn't happen instantly. But if you consistently release the belief you no longer need and hold your new belief in your mind, you will succeed. And from your new beliefs will flow new thoughts and actions that will bring abundance into your life.

Break free of the beliefs that hold you back and give yourself the freedom that beliefs which serve you better can provide.

Secrecy

When you open this book here know that you are keeping, or being asked to keep secrets that you won't benefit from.

What are you hiding from others? What are you too ashamed or embarrassed to talk about? What has someone asked you to keep to yourself that feels uncomfortable?

Secrets are never a good thing. They always create a tension. Secrecy and shame are partners; always to be found together and best avoided.

If you keep a secret it is because you imagine that you will be rejected in some way if you make the information public, or because you are protecting others in an inappropriate way. Do you have a lot of money, and imagine others will be jealous and won't like you for it? Do you have very little, and imagine people will think less of you if they know? Do you have money dealings that are disreputable or underhand? Or perhaps you are unhappy with the way that you earn your money or how you manage it.

The truth is that you need to be true to yourself and know that you can't control the way others respond to you. Trust yourself to handle whatever it is that you need to stop having secrets about.

When you keep secrets about money people will try to guess what is going on and jump to conclusions, often quite wrongly. Be open, above-board, honest and clear. As long as you behave in this way you will feel no need for secrecy or shame. Secrecy attracts negativity to your finances and will do you no good.

Of course you are entitled to privacy. Secrecy and privacy are very different. Privacy involves self-respect and clear boundaries and means that you do not have to make your business public to everyone who asks. Keep it between you and those whom it is appropriate to tell. But do not mistake secrecy for privacy. Secrecy is about hidden information that has shame attached to it whereas privacy is about freely and openly choosing to keep something to yourself.

Refuse to keep secrets and you will earn the respect of others and raise your self-esteem while becoming more comfortable with your own financial situation.

Money Skills

When you open this book here it is because you need greater experience in the handling and management of money, either generally or for something specific that's going on right now.

Many of us grew up with too little understanding of the skills needed for coping with money in our everyday lives. Perhaps we don't even realise that there are skills which are needed for this, and we either feel foolish when we have difficulty in organising our money or feel afraid of having anything to do with money. We assume that others have an automatic grasp of money issues, not realising that it is a learnt skill. Or we acquire a certain set of skills only to find that as life develops we need new skills.

Did you grow up around adults who kept money a mystery? Are you uncomfortable dealing with numbers and don't want to admit it? Did you have parents who managed money badly themselves? As an adult do you dread or avoid keeping accounts, budgeting or even working with the cash in your hand? Or are you so careful around money because the skill that you lack is that of enjoying money?

Perhaps you have difficulties with basic mathematical skills such as subtracting and dividing, whether this comes from poor teaching, lack of confidence or both. Have you learnt to cover up your lack of skill by letting others handle money for you or muddling through with constant excuses? If this is you then it is time to make a different choice. Skills can be learned; experience can be built up. Fears can fall away when you face them.

Sort out what it is you need and find it for yourself. Be truthful about what you can and can't do and what you need to learn in order to manage your money well and without fear. If you are already experienced around money now is the time to develop your skills further. Advance your understanding to a whole new level and watch your financial position flourish. If you are a real avoider around money buy a simple calculator and learn how to use it. Write your money down on paper, don't try to keep it all in your head. Perhaps a friend who is confident about handling money would teach you how to create a simple spending plan. Or you could join an evening class in money management. Or find help and support if you have a problem such as dyslexia.

Take all the energy that you've put into skirting around and avoiding money issues and use it to help yourself to solve your problems around handling money.

Know that you can do it. With courage anything is possible.

Awareness

When you open this book here it is time to focus on your awareness around money matters.

To be aware means to be conscious, knowledgeable and well informed. It means to know and understand what you do with your money and why you do it.

If you are trying to make money changes or a financial decision at the moment, make sure you have all the facts that you need. Bring your full awareness and attention to what you are doing and this will lead to a more successful outcome.

Many of us treat money as a mystery and think of it as fearful, complicated and troublesome. While others do their best not to think about it at all. Does this sound like you? Do you put letters from the bank to one side and try to avoid them? Do you put off looking at your finances and have only a vague idea of what you have or don't have? Do you end up with overdrafts and loans because you spend more than you realise? Do you keep yourself in the dark about your spending and your financial commitments? Recognise that being over-cautious about money and avoiding spending money is about being fearful too.

If so, then know that with awareness it is possible to become comfortable, at ease and relaxed around money. Choose to know what you are doing and why you are doing it and the mystery and unbalanced behaviour around money will disappear.

Get clear and honest with yourself. Find out what you have and what you owe, what you need and what you are going to need. Take advice from people you trust and make informed decisions about what to do with your money. If you have debts get them under control, make a spending plan and stick to it and let go of things that you can't afford. If you have excess, be willing to spend some of it on improving the quality of your life.

Stay aware of your money on an ongoing basis, don't let the fog around money descend again. Keep notes on a day to day basis and review your position every week. If you're thinking of trying something new or different, make sure that you keep yourself aware of exactly what it will entail financially. Avoid being vague. Awareness means clarity and honesty. It doesn't require you to be judgemental, it requires that you have the facts.

When you bring your awareness to all that you do with money you can enjoy the peace of mind which this knowledge and understanding will bring.

Keep it Simple

When you open this book here it is because there is a pressing need to keep things really simple around your finances or any money-related issues.

What is going on that feels complicated or unwieldy? Have you got yourself caught up in all sorts of detail, going backwards and forwards over it without ever finding a resolution that really feels right? Or are you making one decision that feels right one moment only to replace with an alternative as soon as your mood changes a little?

The trouble is that we are experts at complicating things. We get ourselves all caught up with different scenarios, different possibilities and even different strategies for each possibility. We try to anticipate all possible outcomes so that we can feel safe and in control. Know that right now this really isn't necessary. It is simply what we do to try to allay our anxiety, yet actually it's the cause of it. Stop projecting about the future and come into the present. What do you need to do right now, one moment at a time? What is the simplest solution and why are you resisting it and insisting on making things complicated?

When we keep things simple we start to feel the relief and sanity that this brings to our lives and our finances. But we have to be willing to let go of the fog that making things complicated provides for us. When we keep things simple we're much more likely to need to take action around our financial situation whereas making things complicated allows us to procrastinate endlessly while we worry over the details.

Know that simplicity can become your friend. That you'll learn to appreciate its beauty the more you embrace it. That it goes hand in hand with responsibility and independence, since the simple fact is that this is your life and the buck stops with you. You have to provide for yourself and live with the choices that you make.

Keeping it simple may feel scary as it strips away our defences and exposes the need to trust that there is enough in the world and that you will be provided for if you'll put the work into your life in ways that are constructive and productive. It forces you to admit how much of your energy goes into avoidance and excuses and asks you to deal with reality in small doses but consistently.

Keeping it simple is simple and it works. Dare to embrace it now.